Meet Me In The Verses Of My Poems

AF624804

Khadija Alam

BookLeaf Publishing

Presentation by *BookLeaf Publishing*

Web: www.bookleafpub.com

E-mail: info@bookleafpub.com

ISBN: 9789357212175

First edition 2023

DEDICATION

This book is dedicated to my beloved (late) Grandfather, Dada Sahib, Dr. Ziauddin Ahmed Shakeb, who always taught me to rise above the odds and stay forever humble. His existence for me is far beyond that of a grandfather, but a teacher, a friend, and a source of never-ending wisdom. He is the reason I started writing, and he lives on in my words.

1933 - 2021

Meet Me

Meet me where the moon rises
And the sun settles,
Where the fleeting stars
Tell stories of unconditional love,
Meet me in between the verses of my poems
Meet me in the void,
Where silence only delves deeper,
Meet me where you left me,
Incomplete.

Conduit of Poetry

You are the conduit from which my poetry
flows,
The blood which you gifted me unknowingly.
As I stroke my hand over your abandoned
books,
I remember how you would fix their spines,
As if they were human.
Because you've always taught me
The value of knowledge,
The beautiful abyss within every word of a
poem.
You taught me these books will never betray me
Like people do.
You are the reason I write.

Phoenix

Like a phoenix,
You would always rise from the ashes
To be reborn into a magnificent light.
You proved that living in the shadows
Was never an option for you.

Shade of Love

I hope that one day,
Somewhere between the crimson hues
Of the departing sky,
You will discover the true shade of love,
A shade hidden away from rose-tinted epitomes,
A shade deep enough to be felt
But never let you drown,
A shade of love that encapsulates your soul
But lets your heart free,
I hope that one day,
You find that shade of love.

Let go

What are you so afraid of?
Why do you clench your existence
Into the cusp of your hand so tightly,
How will you learn to sway your fingers
With the stir of the bare winds,
How will you learn to let go?

Closure

As I walk through unamended wounds,
Repeat the painful echoes,
That never really left my ears
As the words ‘why me?’ repeat themselves
In unison with my palpating heart,
I ask questions that will probably never be
answered
Staring into the blank distance,
I whisper to myself,
I wish someone had taught me
That closure was a myth.

Cobwebs

It's time to clear those cobwebs in my heart.
The tangled complexities that sat there for a little too long.
The silken threads, binding together, almost like a work of art,
The gathered dust settled perfectly like amassed glitter,
But when I look closer,
I realised,
Those cobwebs have been home to the venomous all along,
So, it's time to clear the cobwebs in my heart,
And say goodbye to those who made a home in my hurt,
For a little too long.

Only Human

I am neither me nor I
I am a mind
I am a body
I am endless
Conversation.
I am a soul
I am an ego
I am unstoppable
Disunion
I am a child
I am an adult
I am an unresolved
Confliction
Above all,
I am only human.

Colony

You create a mosaic of misconceptions
And call it art.
Blurt our eloquent words of subconscious bias
And call to freedom of speech
Block me in paths where you see my radiance
shine
Like the Kohinoor diamond I am,
Wash the colours until they fade because
You fail to see through the pigments of melanin.
You make enough room for me to exist
Yet compress me to the point of suffocation
Because you've always liked me as a colony,
Not a Kingdom.

People & Promises

People will always drop promises
Like falling leaves from an autumn tree,
And wait long enough to say goodbye
Like the summer sun,
People have always been like
The spring that spreads false flowers
And, like the winter,
That never snowed.

Chaos is Art

Let your vulnerability
Cascade down your spine
Let the droplets of uncertainly
Engulf your being
Let the fragments of your mind
Descend to your feet
And remember,
This chaos gave birth to the art
That oozes from your skin.

To The Little Girl I Used To Be

To the little girl, I used to be
I know you're still there somewhere
Yet the world isn't as big as it used to be
I know you'd grow wings to fly beyond
The years to see if it ever got better
Well, here I am, on the other side
Not trying to make songs out of
Memories that never rhymed,
But I'm here to tell you that your gold-plated
tears
Were not valued by those who caused them
So you grew up with an alchemy within you,
An impossible combination of elements,
You have a depth that makes you wise
Yet an inner child, yearning to be loved
You are constantly at odds with the two
So, I'm here to tell you,
That your innocent dreams have always been
important
To me.
You are precious and beautiful.
And when no one is there to tell you that
I will always be
Because that little girl I used to be,
Will always be within me.

Wall

Let the cold breeze
Touch your face
And cool the warming rage
Within you.
Like a feather,
Let it soften the bricks
Of the wall, you have built
So high.

Empathy

She is far from inflexible
She holds her ground
Because she has already
Tossed and turned
Analysed, pulled apart, dreamt and wept
She is far from stubborn
She stays devoted.
Because she has already felt everything in all its entirety
In order to figure you out
And make sure you don't feel a thing,
She is empathy.

Loneliness

Loneliness is not just
The physical absence of someone
It's the spaces where
Your mind lingers
The spaces where
You are consumed by everyone
But accompanied by none.

Broken Souls

Broken souls are not fragile
They are powerful
You won't tear them apart
For, every fragment of their
Shattered pieces
Will only glisten
I like stars in the night sky.

She

Cast shadows all you want
She is the source of her own light
Burn bridges down if you must
It was never her job to help you cross them
Build barriers if you wish
She'll make a home with its walls.

Footprints

As you walk,
You leave footprints of pain
In sands that encompass only bliss
So, may you tread new grounds
And set the way for a path of
Immaculate self-discovery.

Breathe

I’ve only just noticed how
The breeze tickles the treetops
And how the beams of sun
Peak through the spaces
Between the branches
Life has given me a chance
To breathe amidst this beauty.

Rose

Beautiful Strength
Grows like a red roses
From the muddy grounds,
So when you feel like the spirit
To grow cannot be found,
Just remember,
Even delicate petals
Carry so much dirty water
Yet the rose stands tall
No matter what pain
Her thorns have bought her,
Her captivating beauty
Is a symbol of love for all
An emblem of rising effortlessly
After a tragic fall.

Found

Somewhere between
Abundance and scarcity,
I found contentment.

www.ingramcontent.com/pod-product-compliance
Lightning Source LLC
Chambersburg PA
CBHW051721130826
49812CB00034B/1293
* 9 7 8 9 3 5 7 2 1 2 1 7 5 *